IMAGES
of America

MUSTANG
AND THE PONY CAR REVOLUTION

ON THE COVER: NEW YORK WORLD'S FAIR MUSTANG INTRODUCTION. Introducing the Mustang to the public at the 1964 New York World's Fair was partly a matter of luck. Ford Motor Company signed Walt Disney to design the display—a trip through time while riding in a tethered Ford convertible—in 1957, years before a Mustang car was conceived. This publicity photograph shows a bevy of beauties gathered in a new Mustang convertible to tour the exhibit. Another open-top Ford can be seen in line ahead of the Mustang. (Ford Motor Company.)

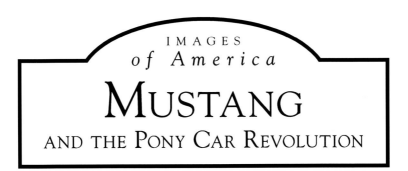

IMAGES
of America

MUSTANG
AND THE PONY CAR REVOLUTION

Michael W.R. Davis

ARCADIA
PUBLISHING

Published by Arcadia Publishing
Charleston, South Carolina

Printed in the United States of America

Library of Congress Control Number: 2013947206

For all general information, please contact Arcadia Publishing:
Telephone 843-853-2070
Fax 843-853-0044
E-mail sales@arcadiapublishing.com
For customer service and orders:
Toll-Free 1-888-313-2665

Visit us on the Internet at www.arcadiapublishing.com

CONTENTS

ACKNOWLEDGMENTS

As it has with a number of my previous Arcadia photographic histories, the National Automotive History Collection at the Detroit Public Library (designated as "N" in the courtesy lines) has been a major source of images for this Mustang history. I am indebted to the following staff members of the library for their assistance with archival resources: Mark Bowden, Paige Plante, Carrie Pruett, and Robert Tate. In addition, Tate (T), a collector himself, supplied information about promotional "toy" Mustangs. And again, Larry Kinsel of GM Media Archives (G) was accommodating in his assistance with GM images, even for a book about its longtime rival, Ford.

When Ford Motor Company initially declined to assist by providing historic images for this book, I sought other sources, including the familiar National Automotive History Collection (NAHC) at the Detroit Public Library, fellow Ford retirees, and photographs I took myself. In early December 2013, as Mustang's half-century anniversary and new product promotion neared, the company invited me to a sneak preview for media and select insiders of the 2015 anniversary car. For this courtesy, I am indebted to Ray Day, Alan Hall, and Jayson Demchak of Ford Communications (FC). Sam Abuelsamid of Team Detroit, Mustang's marketing agency, also provided improved images of late-model Mustangs from Ford's media website.

Others who helped along the way include fellow automotive historians Dr. Charles K. Hyde, Chuck Houser, Mike Skinner, and Jim Wagner (W), and fellow members of the Ford Retired Engineering Executives Club (FREE), especially John Logan (L), Gene Dickirson, and Gale Halderman. Journalists Steve Purdy and Ken Zino, and Christo Datini of the GM Heritage Center also assisted. A "D" indicates my own images, from either my camera or my personal collection, including images from various sources that were keyed in my previous Arcadia automotive histories.

As usual, my wife, Karen, bore up without much companionship from me during the intensive creation of this volume.

INTRODUCTION

In my 25 years with Ford Motor Company Public Relations, I was never a member, specifically, of the Ford Division's PR office, though twice I was "loaned" to the division on special assignments. The first time, my assignment was to prepare press materials for Ford's 1961 truck lines; the second, to prepare all of the US materials for a subcompact Ford of Germany car to be imported for the 1963 model year, internally code-named Cardinal by Ford. This vehicle was to be assembled in Cologne for the European market and in Louisville for the American market.

I had been working diligently for several weeks, preparing the full range of media information on Cardinal and coordinating two simultaneous media previews, scheduled for June 1962, in Germany and in Kentucky. Then, late one afternoon, Walt Murphy, the Ford Division PR chief, came into my borrowed office, lit up his omnipresent pipe when I swiveled to face him, and explained that he had just returned from a round of visiting dealers in Texas with Lee Iacocca, the head of Ford Division. I leaned forward in my chair to receive the gossipy report that made working for Walt so much fun.

"Iacocca's killing the Cardinal," he remarked. All I could blurt out in response was, "No s***?" "Yeah," he continued. "He says 'it's a little old ladies' car, gray on the inside and gray on the outside. We need something with pizzazz to counter Monza.'" Monza was Chevrolet's sporty coupe version of the rear-engine Corvair compact sedan, introduced a couple of years before.

For me, that was the end of Cardinal—almost—and the beginning of Mustang. It turned out that a team of product planners, engineers, stylists, and marketers had been working on a new car concept that, in April 1964, a mere two years later, became the reality of Mustang. This was the start of the pony car revolution. The internal code name for the Mustang, by the way, was "Special Falcon," perhaps because the new sporty coupe was based largely on Falcon components. But I had no role to play in promoting the Mustang, as I was soon assigned to Lincoln-Mercury Division and later to Engineering Staff as a product promotion and information specialist. Over the next two dozen years, however, I did order five Mustangs as my company cars: 1967 six-cylinder manual transmission convertible, yellow with black interior trim and top; 1976 Mustang II white V-6 automatic fastback with red interior; 1979 sister car Mercury Capri, four-cylinder manual, dark green coupe with tan interior; 1984 GT Turbo convertible, red with gray trim and black top, five-speed manual; and 1988 5.0-liter GT convertible, white with red interior, five-speed manual.

At its 1964 introduction, Mustang was presented mainly as a fun car with a low price, sporty features, and a great fuel economy from its six-cylinder Falcon engine. Over the years, it morphed into Ford's right-from-the-showroom-floor muscle or high-performance machine with sticker prices today looming into the $70,000s, more a competitor to Chevrolet's Corvette than, say, to Chevy's own pony car, Camaro, which made its debut two years after the Mustang as a 1967 model. And Plymouth, the third of Detroit's "low-priced" volume car companies, had actually beat the Mustang to market by a couple of weeks, taking the honors for "first pony car" with its glass fastback Barracuda. Mustang stayed in production in one form or another for the ensuing

50 years, while Chrysler discontinued the Plymouth brand in 2001 and GM ceased producing Camaros from 2002 to 2010. The Pontiac brand is gone, along with Mercury and, with them, their pony cars, Firebird and Cougar/Capri.

This history of the Mustang looks to the 1920s, not the early 1960s, for its origins in concept; to the late 1930s for low-cost, fun models and Lincoln Continental styling cues; to the mid-1950s for some of its mechanical and design features; and, finally, to the 1960 Ford Falcon and 1962 Fairlane for components that could be scavenged for the Mustang, to speed it to market and minimize the tooling investment.

There is an old saying that applies perfectly to Mustang: "Success has many fathers; failure is an orphan." Many former Ford executives are credited with being "Father of the Mustang." This book makes no attempt to resolve that debate; indeed, Mustang was a team effort. And many undoubtedly played key roles at one time or another in its success. Few executives, however, claimed key roles in the Edsel fiasco only a few years before Mustang. No doubt, Mustang team members learned—and applied—lessons from the Edsel failure.

This volume is not intended to be a guidebook for Mustang model-to-model changes. For one thing, in some years, there were few or no readily identifiable appearance changes. For another, the age of digitalization has ended the practice of bulky press kits containing black-and-white glossy prints. Now, information and photographs come in tiny flash drives for insertion directly into a computer's hard drive. Moreover, in connection with widespread color printing in magazines and newspapers, the digitized color images tend to be "artistic" (for instance, dark blue car against black background), which don't lend themselves for use in Arcadia Publishing books.

A historian's job is to interpret the facts of a period of time. No doubt, Mustang fans may argue with some of my interpretations. As they say in pari-mutuel betting events, differences of opinion make races—and that's what makes the wagering interesting and exciting.

There are various ways by which the success of a vehicle may be reported: model year (often varies year-to-year and by make), calendar year, retail sales (as reported by news media from manufacturer and importer dealer sources), planning volumes, production (as reported by the automobile manufacturers and published by trade media), import numbers (now rarely used), and new vehicle registrations collected by statistical agencies from state licensing authorities. None are without fault for those doing analysis. In this book, I have sought to use those with year-to-year consistency from reliable sources, mainly production and, for recent years, reported sales.

When Ford Motor Company brings out its 50th-anniversary 2015 Mustang next fall, I hope that this book contributes to the commemoration.

—Michael W.R. "Mike" Davis
Royal Oak, Michigan
December 2013

One

MUSTANG PREWAR PREDECESSORS
1924–1942

HENRY FORD AND 10-MILLIONTH CAR. When the 10-millionth Ford was produced in 1924, Ford Motor Company founder Henry Ford (1863–1947) posed with his "first car," the experimental 1896 Quadricycle (right) and a '24 Touring Car. The earmarked 10-millionth vehicle was launched on a cross-country promotional tour from New York City to San Francisco over the Lincoln Highway—soon to be designated US Highway 30—and, more or less, today's Interstate 80. The car and its tour symbolized how "Old Henry's" mass production of the Model T had revolutionized personal travel worldwide. Without the T's success, there would be no Mustang. (N.)

1924 FORD RUNABOUT. In the author's opinion, the root ancestor of the 1965-model Ford Mustang, introduced on April 17, 1964, was this 1924 Ford Runabout. The Runabout, providing basic transportation for two persons, sold in October 1924 at the lowest price ever for a production motorcar: $260 f.o.b. (without transportation charges) Detroit. In 2013 dollars, that would be $3,552. Cars then did not have model-year designations, and Fords were commonly just "Fords"—not necessarily called "T's," as the replacement Model A was yet four years in the future. The fold-down top on an open car was typical of all American automobiles, little changed from horse-drawn buggies. Compared to modern cars, however, it was "sporty." (N.)

FORD TOURING CAR, 1925. In mid-1925, an "improved Ford" was introduced in reaction to competitive pressure from Chevrolet. As illustrated by the Ford Touring Car shown here, improvements included the addition of a driver's door, lowering the height an inch, steel-wire wheels in place of wooden "artillery wheels," bumpers, and bright-metal headlamps and radiator shell. A year later, in place of Henry Ford's "any color you want as long as it's black" dictum, colors were added, but with choice limited to body style: open cars would be blue or brown; closed cars, green, maroon, or gray. Fenders and running boards remained black. In 1925, for the first time in the automobile industry, closed models outsold open cars in the United States. (N.)

1927 CHEVROLET ADVERTISEMENT. Ford ended Model T production on May 21, 1927, to convert plants for production of the Model A, introduced on December 2, 1927. But in the competition with Chevrolet for the number one sales position, it was too late. For the first time, Chevrolet surpassed Ford in production and, therefore, US sales, a position it held for most of the succeeding years. This Chevy advertisement trumpets "America's all-time favorite since '27." The featured Sports Cabriolet model, a new, "fun" body style of limited practicality, has significance as a spiritual predecessor of the Mustang. (G.)

'32 FORD ROADSTER. This car—a lightweight roadster with an impressive power curve—was the type that Southern California automobile fanatics fashioned into the original "hot rods" in the post–World War II years. The engine was Ford's new 65-horsepower, 221-cubic-inch V-8, introduced on March 1, 1932. With rumble seat, this car sportily carried four occupants. (W.)

'37 FORD DELUXE CABRIOLET. In the 1930s, Ford picked up where Chevrolet left off, offering hand-operated convertible-top roadsters with and without rumble seats. Ford also sold a "Club" convertible with an enclosed back seat—in other words, a total "fun" car, and sporty, too. This 1937 Ford convertible with the top up shows the huge advance in "streamlined" styling, compared to cars of the previous decade. (N.)

'39 FORD DELUXE CABRIOLET. This 1939 Ford convertible with rumble seat, shown in owner Jack Roush's extensive private collection in Livonia, Michigan, is a fitting ancestor of the Mustang. The '39 is sporty, though relatively impractical in an era of cavernous sedans. The Roush collection features two of these '39 ragtops. No convertibles were offered in Ford's lower-priced 1939 Standard series. (D.)

'39 FORD V-8 ENGINE. The 1939 "flathead" Ford 221-cid, 85-horsepower V-8 shown here was the principal power plant for Ford cars from 1932 through 1953. Beginning in 1937, a smaller, 136-cid, 60-horsepower V-8 was used in Ford's European-assembled cars and trucks and "Standard" series American Fords. In response to competition, the 221 V-8 had seen its horsepower increased several times since its 1932 introduction. (D.)

'39 FORD RUMBLE SEAT ROADSTER. The '39 Ford shown here with top down and rumble seat open was the last US car to offer a rumble seat roadster model. Chevrolet produced no convertibles in the United States for 1939, while Plymouth introduced the first power-operated convertible top. The two steps on the right rear of this unquestionably sporty $790 '39 Ford convertible provided access to the two-place rumble seat. (D.)

'39 FORD ROADSTER. When the rumble seat was neatly closed, as seen here, the space could be used for carrying small amounts of cargo or luggage. Rumble-seat passengers otherwise enjoyed both fresh air and protection from chilly weather, as their legs fit underneath the body behind the front seats. (D.)

'39 LINCOLN-ZEPHYR CONVERTIBLE. This catalog illustration shows the $1,700 1939-model Lincoln-Zephyr convertible, on which Edsel Ford's custom car (below) was based. It was powered by Lincoln's 267.5-cid flathead V-12 engine, rated at 110 horsepower. This production Lincoln-Zephyr was mounted on a 125-inch wheelbase, but it was 3.5 inches higher than both the custom '39 Continental and the 1940 models. (W.)

CUSTOM '39 LINCOLN-ZEPHYR CONVERTIBLE. In the design of Edsel Ford's customized 1939 Lincoln-Zephyr (the one-of-a-kind "first" Continental), the hood was lengthened by seven inches, the body sectioned (lowered) three or four inches, the passenger compartment moved rearward, and the trunk shortened to create the unique "continental" appearance seen here. This joint creative effort by Edsel himself and designer Eugene T. "Bob" Gregorie provided an inside-Ford styling legacy for later-production Thunderbirds, the mid-1950s Continental Mark II, and the 1965 Mustang. (N.)

'40 LINCOLN CONTINENTAL CONVERTIBLE AND COUPE. The limited-production 1940 Continental convertible (above) was derived from Edsel's '39 custom job (opposite page). Based on the Lincoln-Zephyr, 350 such Continental convertibles were produced, nearly seven times as many as the 54 1940-model coupes (below). The LC coupes were premium priced at $2,840, compared to a Lincoln-Zephyr club coupe at $1,400. The 292-cubic-inch V-12 engine was larger than that of the '39s, but the chassis was the same. A highly visible change from Edsel's custom 1939 car was the steel cover for the spare tire. The 1940 Continental coupe established a new style for steel top two-door models, followed by later Continentals and eventually Mustang's notchback models. (Both, N.)

'41 LINCOLN CONTINENTAL CONVERTIBLE. The 1941 Continental Cabriolet convertible pictured here shows few changes from the 1940 models illustrated on the previous page, the modifications limited mainly to push-button door latches (instead of handles) and parking lamps atop the front fenders. Priced at $2,778 (a slight reduction), 1941 production increased to 400 convertibles and 850 coupes. Importantly, the long hood and short rear deck continued, establishing the design theme for future Continentals, some upper series Ford sedans (Galaxie), and the Mustang. (N.)

Two
MUSTANG POSTWAR PREDECESSORS
1945–1960

'46 LINCOLN CONTINENTAL COUPE. After World War II, Continental's design continued, with carryover styling details from 1942 models. This is a rear view of the squared-off postwar Lincoln Continental model. Indeed, the American and European auto industries' initial postwar models had carryover designs from prewar times. Lincoln's mechanical specifications were the same as for 1942 models, featuring a 130-horsepower, 305-cid V-12 engine, larger than those of the 1940 and 1941 models. Lincoln's 1942 experimental automatic transmission, called Liquamatic, was dropped. (N.)

EXPERIMENTAL CHEVROLET CADET. Across town in 1945, Chevrolet's Engineering Department—its war work completed—was developing a "Light Car" called the Cadet (shown here). GM aborted the program in 1947 because a long postwar United Auto Worker strike and material shortages threatened timely introduction of the larger standard Chevrolet for 1949. But a number of Cadet's experimental mechanical developments were transferred to Ford and, eventually, to the Mustang by engineers seeking new opportunities. The Cadet, designed to carry four occupants, would be powered by a 65-horsepower OHV, 133-cid, six-cylinder engine (smaller but similar to the prevailing Chevy's 216.5-cid). (G.)

'53 FORD SUSPENDED PEDALS. Suspended brake and clutch pedals, seen at lower left, were among the innovations developed at GM for the discontinued Cadet. The '52 Ford presented an all-new body and interior design, which made it relatively easy for former GM engineers at Ford to accommodate designs from the GM concept into a different size and make car. This is a 1953 Ford with carryover design from the prior model year. (N.)

'48 MG. A major influence on Mustang was the growing popularity of relatively low-cost imported sports cars, led by this MG TC British car, featuring a long hood and short rear deck. Bucket seats and floor-mounted shifters were other important features of imported sports cars. Though sales of all imports were then modest, MG was the third-most-popular import (after Austin and English Ford) in the late 1940s. The 1,735-pound TC was priced at $2,238, when the lowest-price domestic 1948 Ford, at 3,033 pounds, was $1,152, and a Continental topped out at $4,746. (N.)

'50 JAGUAR XK-120. At the high-priced end of such imports was the $3,945 XK-120 Jaguar, its top and side curtains fastened against wet weather. The premium-priced imported sports car was typified in 1950 by this Jaguar roadster, popularized by European road-race standings and its sleek design, again offering long hood and short deck. But it was all relative: a little more than 900 Jaguars of all types were sold in the United States in 1950, rising to 3,349 in 1952, when US sales of all cars exceeded four million. (N.)

'51 VW CABRIOLET. Sales of VW Beetles, like this vintage 1951 Cabriolet (convertible) model, shown during a Meadowbrook Concours car show, began modestly, with only 550 in 1951, rising to about 29,000 in 1955. Note the slot in the cowl forward of the VW driver door, which housed a European-type turn signal. VW Beetles first imported to America featured rear-mounted, air-cooled engines, a concept adopted less successfully by Chevrolet Corvairs in the 1960s. (D.)

'52 NASH-HEALEY. America's first sports car, the Nash-Healey, debuted at the Chicago Auto Show in February 1951. It was a three-way project of George Mason of Nash-Kelvinator, British sports-car builder Sir Donald Healey, and Italian designer Pininfarina. The car was assembled in Warwick, England, with a modified Nash sedan's enhanced six-cylinder overhead valve engine. When Nash and Hudson merged in mid-1954, the sports car's production ceased after a four-year build of only 506 units. (N.)

'54 KAISER DARRIN. Following the Nash adventure, the relatively new Kaiser-Frazer Motors produced this one-year Kaiser Darrin roadster for 1954. Like the Chevrolet Corvette shown below, the Darrin featured a fiberglass body. Engines, however, originated with either Continental Motors Sixes, designed for the larger Kaiser sedans, or carryover Jeep truck Sixes. Production of the Darrin totaled only 435. (N.)

'53 CORVETTE. The fiberglass-bodied Chevrolet Corvette created a sensation when first shown at GM's Motorama exhibition at New York's Waldorf-Astoria Hotel in January 1953. GM reacted quickly, with output at the Chevrolet Flint assembly plant beginning on June 30. Calendar year 'Vette production totaled only 300, all powered by a troublesome triple-carburetor Six, a modified Chevy passenger car engine with Powerglide automatic transmission. Corvette's racing performance did not begin until the small-block V-8 became available for 1955. (N.)

'55 THUNDERBIRD CONVERTIBLE. Ford also reacted quickly to the perceived new market for sports cars, introducing the steel-bodied, two-place Thunderbird (shown here) in February 1954, barely a year after Corvette's debut. Note the relatively long hood and short deck, similar conceptually to Lincoln Continental and its "greenhouse," a forerunner to the Mustang. Initially, the Thunderbird was available, like Corvette, only as a convertible. (N.)

'55 THUNDERBIRD COUPE. This rear view of a two-place T-Bird, as the car came to be known, shows the closed (windowless) rear quarter of the car's optional removable top, a styling feature originating with the Continental coupes of the 1940s that was continued in future Ford Motor Company cars, especially the '56 Continental Mark II, later T-Birds, and, ultimately, the Mustang. For '57s, a porthole in the rear sides of the top was added. (N.)

'56 CONTINENTAL MARK II. The 1956 Continental Mark II was produced in 1956 and 1957 as a two-door coupe only, lending itself readily to the established long-hood, short-deck design first seen with the original custom Continental of 1939. Mark II production over the two years totaled just 3,000. Priced at $10,000, at the time, Mark II was America's highest-priced production car. Dubbing this Continental a "Mark II" automatically made its predecessors of the 1940s "Mark Ones." (N.)

'58 THUNDERBIRD. Whereas the two-place T-Birds of 1955–1957 had readily outsold the rival Chevrolet Corvette (21,380 to 6,339 in 1957), Ford Division planners calculated that if the model were enlarged to carry four occupants, sales would increase even more. In the recession year of 1958, the new T-Bird counted production of 37,982 (versus Corvette's 9,168), rising to 92,798 by 1960. This success greatly influenced the planners, resulting in Mustang's original design being stretched to accommodate four occupants. (N.)

'60 Falcon Two-Sided "Styling Clay." Reacting to rapidly increasing imported-car sales, Ford, GM, and Chrysler went to work developing "small cars" for October 1959 introduction of the 1960 model year. Careful analysis of this image shows a Falcon four-door sedan on the far side and a two-door model on the near side. Two-sided clay models were a conventional styling staff approach used in early management reviews and consumer "clinics" to rate design proposals. (N.)

'60 Falcon Two-Door Sedan. This is a front-quarter view of the two-door Falcon sedan. Selling for $1,974, it was the lowest-priced of Ford's new "compact" cars. It weighed 2,317 pounds on a 109.5-inch wheelbase, with an overall length of 181.2 inches, versus the standard full-sized Ford sedan at 3,605 pounds and $2,311. The two-door sedan was, with production of 193,470, the top-selling Falcon in 1960. (N.)

'60 FALCON FOUR-DOOR SEDAN. The second-best-selling Falcon for 1960 was this four-door sedan, of which 167,896 were produced. The standard engine was a 144-cid, 85-horsepower overhead-valve Six, manufactured at an Ohio Ford engine plant erected a few years earlier to make V-8 engines for the ill-fated Edsel. Ford had abandoned the Edsel with huge losses late in 1959. Falcon's small Six provided excellent fuel economy, but already the public was perceived as demanding more power. The Falcon was designed to carry six occupants, two more than the ill-fated Chevrolet Cadet, developed 15 years earlier. In addition to the two sedans, Falcon offered a $2,225 two-door and a $2,287 four-door station wagon. The wagons were, at 189 inches, slightly longer than the sedans. Standard—soon to be called "big"—Ford sedans were mounted on 119-inch wheelbases and were 213.7 inches long. The big Fords were also wider than their compact siblings, measuring 81.5 inches. (N.)

'60 MERCURY COMET. The Comet was a sister car to the Falcon, offered by Lincoln-Mercury dealers beginning midyear, March 17, 1960. Internally, it had been known as the "Edsel B," evidently intended to assist bereft Edsel dealers. This photograph shows 1960 Comets at an assembly plant, where they were made on the same line as Falcons. Comet sedans rode on a longer (114-inch) wheelbase than the Falcon and sold at premium prices, ranging from $1,998 to $2,365. (N.)

'60 CORVAIR FOUR-DOOR. Initially, the rear-engine Corvair was offered in just two body styles, this four-door sedan, and a two-door coupe, and in three series, 500, 700, and 900. Prices ranged from $1,984 to $2,238. It went on sale six days before Ford's Falcon. The engine was a 140-cid opposed-cylinder OHV Six of 80 horsepower with an aluminum block—very radical among American cars. Corvair's total production of 1960 models came to 250,000. (N.)

'60 Corvair Coupe. The Corvair coupe shown here was as close to a Porsche as Chevrolet general manager Edward Cole could make it. In the upper 900 series, the coupe was labeled a Monza. The Monza, a late starter in the model year, elicited the most enthusiastic support, including Motor Trend's Car of the Year award. Its very success convinced Ford Division's general manager, Lee Iacocca, that Ford needed a sporty economy car. (N.)

'60 Valiant Four-Door Sedan. Chrysler took a design tack between the conventional Falcon and the radical Corvair. The styling actually elicited applause from journalists at the introductory news conference, and the car offered a number of technical advances. Valiant had an unusual Slant Six OHV engine of 101 horsepower and 171 cubic inches and the first alternator in place of a generator. (N.)

'60 VALIANT WAGON. Valiant's other body style for the 1960 model was this compact station wagon. So, American automobile shoppers could select from an unusual variety of "compact cars" in 1960. Valiant's production for the year came to 194,292, well below that of Corvair and Falcon. Prior to the 1960 model year, the air around Detroit had been filled with speculation about the forthcoming "small cars." In addition to the three new sizes of cars from Big Three industry leaders General Motors, Ford, and Chrysler, independents American Motors and Studebaker-Packard also offered "compact" cars. Nonetheless, the import invasion led by VW continued to increase its percentage of the new car market. The first result was product proliferation, wherein the Big Three went from a single size (large) to several sizes in the 1960s, and then to a whole new type of entry: the pony car. Curiously, there was little speculation about the Mustang before its introduction, in contrast to much before the compact-car craze. (N.)

Three

PRE-INTRODUCTION MUSTANG TEASERS
1961–1964

'63 CARDINAL V-4 POWER PACK. Ford had been planning a 1963-model US introduction of a subcompact-sized German Ford, code-named Cardinal. In the belief that the European and US markets wanted an economical car with a high-tech engine—to engage the Corvair and the VW Beetle—the Cardinal would have an unusual V-4 engine in combination with front-wheel-drive, as seen in the "power pack" illustrated here. For the European market, it was branded Taunus 12M. (N.)

US Cardinal. The front-drive Cardinal, shown here in its prototype US version, was virtually identical to the Taunus 12M, successfully produced for years in its mother country. But for the United States, Lee Iacocca called the Cardinal a "little old lady's car, gray on the outside and gray on the inside" and ordered the project killed in April 1962. A few months after the British Ford Cortina and 12M were introduced, Ford of Europe was created to merge Ford's British and German companies, thereby eliminating costly development of separate but similar cars. (N.)

FORD OF GERMANY TAUNUS 12M. In Europe, several different body styles of the Taunus 12M/ Cardinal were offered, like the sporty coupe in the above photograph and the station wagon model shown below. In the United States, Ford Division planned to offer only the two-door sedan shown on the previous page. The division's product development team rushed on a replacement car; the Mustang launched just two years later. (Both, N.)

FORD OF BRITAIN CORTINA. Code-named "Archbishop," in association with Ford of Germany's "Cardinal," the rear-drive Cortina was imported for sale by Lincoln-Mercury dealers beginning in late 1963. It continued to be offered in North America until it was replaced by the German-built Capri sports coupe in 1969. The street-legal race car Cortina Lotus also was imported in the 1960s. Visible in the below photograph are the typical US Ford round taillights. (Both, N.)

MUSTANG I. Just six months before sales were to begin, Iacocca decided to abandon the Cardinal program and invest in a sporty all-American car instead. But Ford Public Relations had "purchased" (via intercompany transfer of budgeted funds) a Cardinal for media preview publicity purposes, and that prototype was hurriedly converted to a "dream car," tagged "Mustang." It is shown here with Herbert Misch, vice president, Engineering and Research (left) and Eugene Bordinat, vice president, Design. The little two-seater, unveiled at the Watkins Glen sports-car racetrack in October 1963, became an unplanned teaser to excite expectation about a future Ford model. (N.)

MUSTANG I COCKPIT. As noted on the previous page, Ford's Dearborn research engineers converted the prototype Cardinal "press car" to a "dream car," the Mustang I. The engineers changed the car from a front-drive to a mid-engine model, reversing the engine and transmission to be mounted behind the passenger compartment. This photograph shows the sports-car-like cockpit of the Mustang I, of which two were built. Only one had all the mechanical components. This operable dream car was donated to the Henry Ford Museum in Dearborn. (N.)

CARDINAL/TAUNUS 12M. This photograph shows the production German car's austere interior. The gearshift lever is mounted on the steering column, as had been American practice since before World War II. The contrast with the sporty Mustang I panel above, with its floor shift, is striking. (N.)

'62 FALCON FUTURA. To counteract buyer interest in the Chevrolet Corvair Monza coupe, in mid-1961, this Falcon Futura was introduced. It was a mundane two-door sedan, but it offered bucket seats, a center console to hold the manual or automatic transmission selector, and upgraded trim. By 1962, the 144-cid engine of 1960 could be replaced with an optional longer-stroke, 101-horsepower, 170-cid version. (N.)

'62 FORD FAIRLANE. Ford's big product news for the 1962 model year was the introduction of the intermediate-size Fairlane, available as two-door and four-door sedans and four-door station wagon. With a wheelbase of 115.5 inches and an overall length of 197.6 inches, the intermediate was close to the 1949 Ford in dimensions, and offered a choice of the 170-cid Six or a new 221-cid V-8 engine. Prices ranged from $2,154 to $2,607, and 1962 production came to 217,510. The addition of the Fairlane provided both more common parts with the forthcoming Mustang and lower amortization costs. (N.)

"MEDIAN" DREAM CAR. Because of Mustang I showings, enthusiast attention turned to speculation about whether the Cardinal-based "dream" car might become a production car. So, Ford's design staff began experimenting with various designs for company executives to consider for a future sporty car. This is one of the earliest of the speculative designs, known as the "Median" and dating from the 1961–1962 period. Its appearance was based on elements of both the two- and four-place Thunderbirds of the 1950s. (N.)

ALLEGRO, FRONT VIEW. The Allegro was another of several "dream" show cars developed by Ford Design Staff as part of the buildup for introduction of the 1965 Mustang. Photographs were distributed to the public, and the Allegro was displayed at various automotive events around the country. Only the grille design seems to have influenced the subsequent production Mustang, which had a very different rear appearance. (N.)

ALLEGRO, REAR VIEW. The c. 1962 rear view of the Allegro dream car (above) shows the round tail lamps common to Ford Division cars since 1952 models, except for 1958. Another version of the fastback show car (below, on a test track) has a different rear end, with pairs of segmented, squarish tail lamps, which evolved into a long-lasting Mustang marker. It is not known which fastback came first, and whether it influenced the three-segment rear-light signature of Mustangs in subsequent years. (N.)

MUSTANG I DREAM CAR. Here again is the Mustang I dream car, on display at the Henry Ford Museum in Dearborn. The car in the museum was fully drivable, but another Mustang I (see page 35) was fashioned only with a fiberglass body and full trim, without an engine and transmission. For many years, it was displayed at Ford's Scientific Research Lobby, but its fate is unknown. (D.)

"COUGAR" DREAM CAR. This was the final operable dream car from Design Center as part of the Mustang tease. Originally dubbed "Cougar" and, later, Mustang II, it closely resembled the production Mustang, except that the greenhouse is cut lower with a more slanted windshield, and the front end is very different. The Cougar/Mustang II was donated to the Detroit Historical Museum in the 1970s and has been displayed, kept in storage, or loaned to other museums since. (N.)

Four

MUSTANG LAUNCH
APRIL 1964

HENRY FORD II AT NEW YORK WORLD'S FAIR. Henry Ford II, chairman of the board of the Ford Motor Company and eldest grandchild of the company's founder, poses here outside the Ford pavilion at the 1964 New York World's Fair. The Mustang officially went on sale Tuesday, April 17, 1964, but Ford unveiled its new car to the news media on Friday, April 13. Henry Ford II's involvement with Mustang consisted mainly of approving the project at various points along its development and, importantly, agreeing to allocate $75 million to the program. (FC.)

41

Ford Mustang Hardtop with Vinyl-Covered Roof

Presenting
the unexpected...
new Ford Mustang!
$2368* f.o.b. Detroit

This is the car you never expected from Detroit. Mustang is so distinctively beautiful it received the Tiffany Award for Excellence in American Design... the first time an automobile has been honored with the Tiffany Gold Medal. Mustang has the look, the fire, the flavor of the great European road cars. Yet it's as American as its name and as practical as its price—just $2,368 f.o.b. Detroit . . . and we're not fooling! This price includes these luxury features that are unavailable or available only at extra cost in most other makes of cars: bucket seats, padded instrument panel, full wheel covers, all-vinyl interior, and wall-to-wall carpeting.

$2,368 f.o.b. Detroit also includes, as standard equipment: sports steering wheel, 3-speed transmission with floor shift, cigarette lighter, front arm rests, two automatic courtesy lights and glove box light.

✱ $2,368 f.o.b. Detroit is the suggested retail price. It does not include, of course, destination charges

MUSTANG INTRODUCTORY ADVERTISEMENT. This is one of several similar Mustang introductory advertisements released on April 13, 1964, in this case, a full-color, two-page spread placed in weekly and monthly magazines. It broadcasts the relatively low price for such a sporty car, $2,368, and further, the advertisement proceeds to identify "upscale" options, such as whitewall tires ($33.90) and vinyl roof ($75.80). The advertisement also suggests various options—air-conditioning, power

from Detroit, options, state and local taxes and fees, if any. Whitewalls are $33.90 extra and the vinyl roof covering is $75.80 extra.

The basic Mustang is an eminently practical and economical car. With its four-passenger room, and surprisingly spacious trunk, it's as much car as many people will ever want or need. But—Mustang was designed to be designed by you. You can fit out your Mustang to almost any degree of luxury or high performance by selecting from a large but reasonably priced group of options.

You can go the luxury route by choosing such options as air conditioning, a push-button radio, vinyl roof covering, power brakes, power steering, 3-speed Cruise-O-Matic transmission—you name it.

Or, your Mustang can become a sports car with the addition of the big 289-cu. in. V-8 engine (the same basic V-8 that powers the famous Cobra!), 4-speed stick shift (synchro in all forward speeds), and Rally Pac (tachometer and clock).

Ford Mustang Convertible

TRY <u>TOTAL PERFORMANCE</u>
FOR A CHANGE!

FORD

Mustang · Falcon · Fairlane · Ford · Thunderbird

For an exciting, authentic scale model of the new Ford Mustang, send $1.00 to Ford Offer, Department F,. P.O. Box 35, Troy, Michigan. (Offer ends July 31, 1964)

brakes, and automatic transmission—to make a Mustang "luxurious." Other options—289 V-8 engine and floor-mounted four-speed transmission—offered a "sporty" Mustang. The side-view image emphasizes the long hood and short rear deck of the Mustang. The advertisement at once displays both the coupe and the convertible models initially offered. (D.)

CONFIDENTIAL

FALCON, FAIRLANE, FORD, THUNDERBIRD, AND NOW....

THE NEW FORD

MUSTANG

TECHNICAL INFORMATION FOR PRESS USE ONLY
FOR RELEASE PM'S APRIL 13, 1964

REGISTRATION NO.

ADVANCE MUSTANG PRESS PACKET. This is the cover of the "long-lead" press packet for monthly magazines that had to be carefully distributed as early as mid-January 1964, more than three months before actual release, due to print scheduling. This required detailed coordination with advertising, distribution of dealership information (for customer ordering), and the World's Fair media introduction. To be successful, secrecy about the heralded new car had to be maintained—especially its appearance. Remarkably, there were few or no leaks of this material—say from a monthly publication to a daily newspaper or weekly magazine—as all parties privy to the information kept the trust, fearing that otherwise they might be excluded from timely access to news in the future. (D.)

MUSTANG MAGAZINE COVERS. This is a collage of weekly and monthly magazine covers announcing the Mustang. The two national newsweeklies, *Time* and *Newsweek*, featured covers with Ford Division chief Lee Iacocca and the Mustang. Rival magazines having the same cover in the same week, particularly of a commercial product, was unheard of. Bringing off this "coup" was a mark of the skill of Ford's publicists. But Mustang did not fare so well with the major automotive consumer magazine of the time, *Motor Trend*, whose cover featured the Plymouth Barracuda, in part because Barracuda's announcement date was set, cleverly, two weeks earlier than Mustang's. (D.)

EARLY MUSTANG BEING TESTED. According to *Mustang Genesis* author Robert Fria, last-minute product changes were being incorporated on the Mustang up to a few weeks prior to public introduction. This Mustang convertible is being tested on a Ford proving ground high-speed track. Note that there is no Mustang emblem in the grille. Evidently, the exact emblem of a running horse was still lacking final approval at the time this undated photograph was taken. (N.)

MUSTANG GRILLE. Shown here is the final "running horse" emblem and logo as it was mounted in the center of the grille of a 1965 Mustang. The logo, whether located on the front quarter panels or elsewhere, continued to this day. During the car's initial development, there were at least two logo proposals and, likewise, some dispute over the new sporty car's brand name. (N.)

INTRODUCING THE MUSTANG. Finally, the big day came, the culmination of two to three years of intensive management attention in a new concept for popular-priced automobiles. Here, Ford Motor Company vice president and Ford Division general manager Lee A. Iacocca presents the Mustang to the automotive and general news press corps in the Ford Pavilion at the New York World's Fair on Friday, April 13, 1964. The official "on-sale" date for the Mustang was four days later, and the fair itself did not open to the general public until April 22. (N.)

'65 MUSTANG PRESS PHOTOGRAPH. One of many press-release photographs distributed by Ford Division announcing the new Mustang was this image tying the car to the horse. In part, this was to establish that the car was named after the animal, rather than the World War II US Army Air Corps North American P-51 fighter aircraft, the Mustang. The car's fans, particularly those enthusiastic about its high-speed performance, preferred to associate it with the P-51. (N.)

PLASTIC MODEL MUSTANGS. For many decades, it has been customary for automobile companies to license toy makers to make small-scale (6- to 8.5-inch-long) plastic replicas of new models. These are sold by dealers or other merchants for $1 to $2 each or distributed as gifts. As a member of the news media and, later, a Ford public relations man, the author collected a variety of such models, but no Mustangs. Some of these models—for instance, special-event models adorned with decals denoting the event—can command as much as $1,000 from hobbyists and collectors. Shown above is a model of the 1965 Mustang, once worth $2 but now commanding $135 in perfect condition with its original box. Below is a model of the 2+2 Fastback Mustang. (Both, D.)

Toy Mustang. As shown on this and the preceding pages, Ford was successful in attracting toy manufacturers to produce scaled-down models of the Mustang. Here is a $4.95 battery-powered Mustang, larger than the plastic promotional models available from Ford dealers, but obviously smaller than the pedal cars (below) for kids slightly older. (T.)

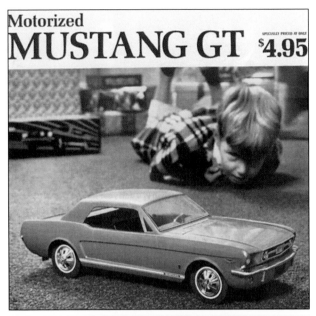

Mustang Pedal Car. Ford arranged for a pedal-car manufacturer to produce and market mechanical Mustang-appearing pedal cars for those not old enough for bicycles and far too young for driver's licenses. Here, Detroit Ford dealer Al Long is pictured with what he hopes will be two future customers. The author's grown daughter still has fond memories of her first red Mustang pedal car, a Christmas 1964 gift. (N.)

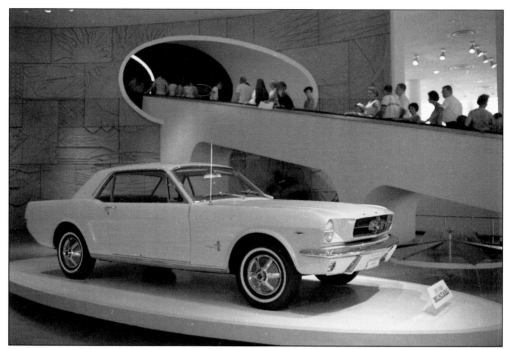

'65 MUSTANG COUPE. Amid other promotions to create awareness and desire, Mustangs had high visibility at the New York World's Fair. The 1964–1965 fair was located in Flushing Meadows, a public park in Queens, site of the 1939–1940 New York World's Fair. Here, a Mustang coupe is displayed at the Ford Pavilion, where a long line of visitors cannot miss seeing it as they progress into the pavilion's displays. (FC.)

'65 MUSTANG CONVERTIBLE. Outside the Ford Pavilion, a Mustang convertible, the second body style on sale soon after the April 17 public introduction, also had high visibility. When this photograph was taken, rainy weather must have been threatening, as the convertible's top is in the up, or closed, position. However, as shown on the cover of this book, there were other top-down convertible versions available for fair visitors to ride in on the Trip Through Time of the Disney-designed exhibit. (FC.)

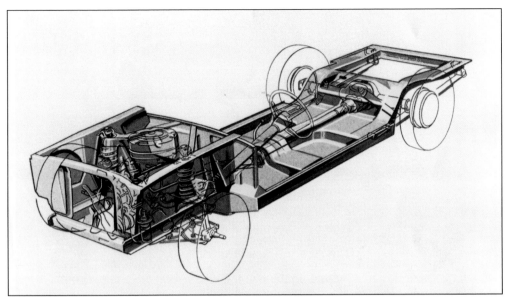

INNER BODY PANELS. One of the secrets of the Mustang's relatively short, two-year development period at minimum cost was the fact that inner body panels of the 1960 Falcon and 1962 Fairlane could be used with only minor tweaking for the 1965 Mustang. This drawing shows some of these body components: engine compartment inner panels, engine/suspension support, frame rails, and floor pan. (N.)

'65 MUSTANG COUPE. In the weeks following the formal Mustang press preview on April 13, 1964, Ford publicists distributed a large variety of the new car's photographs to print media. This photograph, a left-side view of a "notchback" hardtop (pillarless) coupe, is part of a set called "reference photos" of front, side, and rear of each new car. Motion picture releases were issued to television and movie news outlets as well. (N.)

'65 Mustang Reference Photographs. Among the photographs seen here is, at lower left, an unglamorous straight-on front view of the new Mustang. As for all new model cars, such reference photographs as this and the one on the preceding page were also distributed to law enforcement agencies for identification purposes. Initial Mustang production took place at Dearborn Assembly Plant in the Rouge, or Ford River Rouge Complex. When demand zoomed, Mustang assembly was added at San Jose, California, in July 1964 and Metuchen, New Jersey, in February 1965. (N.)

Air-Conditioning and Automatic Transmission. In the realm of "creature comforts" were the optional $283 air-conditioning and $180 automatic transmission, shown in this photograph of a Mustang interior. Note that the air-conditioning unit (just forward of the automatic transmission control) is "hang-on," because the instrument panel had not yet (as of this 1966 model) been redesigned to incorporate AC components. (N.)

'65 MUSTANG INSTRUMENT PANEL. Shown here is the design of a different 1965 Mustang interior, notably, the cockpit of a "performance" model equipped with optional four-speed manual transmission ($116 with Six, $76 with V-8), full-length center console ($52), and a "Rally-Pac" of tachometer and clock ($71). Other performance-related options included limited-slip differential ($43), front disc brakes ($58), power brakes ($43), and three different V-8 engines (with prices up to $443 extra). Many options in '65s became standard equipment in later model years, with their costs rolled into higher prices for the total vehicle. Some, such as instrument-panel padding and seat belts, resulted directly or indirectly from Federal Motor Vehicle Safety Standards. (N.)

170-CID SIX ENGINE. Mustang's base engine when the car went on sale in April 1964 was this 101-horsepower, 170-cubic-inch OHV Six, also offered as the well-proven base engine in several other Ford compact and midsized cars. The engine was upsized from the 144-cubic-inch version that powered Falcon at its 1960 model introduction. Later in the year, a slightly larger, 116-horsepower, 200-cid Six became standard in Mustang. Sixes accounted for 49 percent of initial Mustang production, later dipping to 36 percent. (N.)

260-CID V-8 ENGINE. The first step up in optional-at-extra-cost engines at Mustang's introduction was this 164-horsepower, 260-cid V-8 power plant, upsized from the 221-cid engine originally designed for the midsized 1962 Ford Fairlane sedan. Even more powerful Mustang V-8s were two slightly larger engines of 289-cid, the first producing 210 horsepower and, later in the year, a "high-performance" 289 boasting 271 horsepower. Numerous options allowed buyers to tailor their Mustangs for versions from economy to luxury to high performance. (N.)

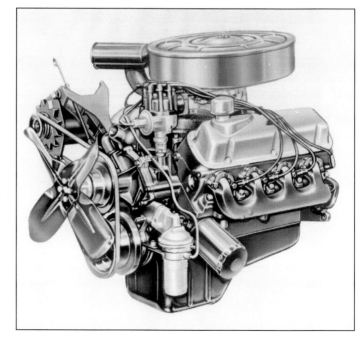

'65 MUSTANG FRONT SUSPENSION. The drawing at right illustrates the basic Short/Long Arm (SLA) Four-Link front suspension standard in Mustang, with shock absorbers enclosed by front coil springs mounted on the upper arm, adapted from the Falcon suspension system. The below photograph shows the underside of the 1965 Mustang front suspension. The later (1979) Fox Mustang used a modified McPherson strut with the spring on the lower arm rather than on the strut, as in an original McPherson strut used on many small foreign cars, including several European Fords. (Both, N.)

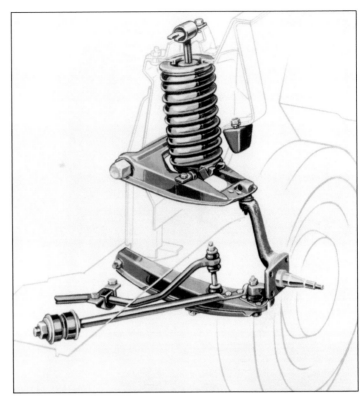

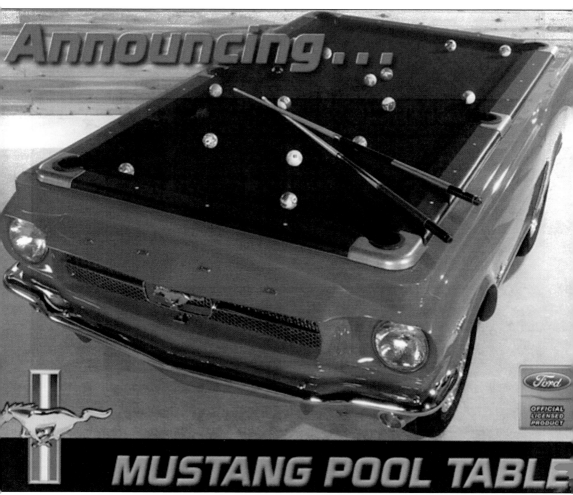

MUSTANG POOL TABLE. Interest remains high in original 1965 Mustangs. For example, Ford has licensed a Florida company since 2008 to manufacture the Mustang pool table shown here, priced at $9,995. In another form of sales promotion, Ford's Studio Car Program contracted to supply cars for the third James Bond movie, *Goldfinger*, shipping a Mustang convertible to Europe before public introduction for what turned out to be no more than a cameo role. However, a 1968 Mustang 390 played a major Hollywood role, thanks to a memorable four-minute San Francisco chase scene in the movie *Bullitt*, staring Steve McQueen. Some 20 years later, Ford marketed a modern Bullitt replica Mustang in the same color. (T.)

Five

MUSTANG ROLLOUT
TO 1966

BENSON FORD AT INDY 500. Benson Ford, younger brother of Henry Ford II, drove a new Mustang convertible as the pace car in the 1964 Memorial Day (May 31) Indianapolis 500 race. Here, he is shown relaxing in the pace car in front of the grandstand at the finish line. For many years, Benson was the Ford family's and the company's ambassador to the auto-racing community and Ford dealers. (N.)

'64 FALCON AND '65 MUSTANG. Among the many photographs distributed in connection with Mustang's introduction was this comparison shot of a 1964 Falcon Futura two-door hardtop (left) and a Mustang convertible, which was based on Falcon mechanicals. Hardtop and convertible body styles had been added to the Falcon line in 1963, along with optional V-8 engines. (N.)

'65 MUSTANG CONVERTIBLE. According to industry records, 101,945 Mustang convertibles were produced for the formal 1965 model year. This would have constituted about 18 percent of total output, a relatively high proportion. In recent years, convertibles have hovered around 5 percent of the new car market. Disagreements occur regarding production numbers for the Mustang, as enthusiasts distinguish between the "1964 1/2" and the "1965" models. (N.)

'65 CONVERTIBLE COCKPIT. The full open-air feel of a Mustang convertible is illustrated in this overhead view. The 1965 Mustang was mounted on a 108-inch wheelbase with an overall length of 181.6 inches, compared to the Falcon's 109.5-inch wheelbase and 181.1-inch length. Both were 68 inches in overall width. This photograph emphasizes the Mustang's roominess, despite the car's cozy rear seat, which comfortably held only two adults. (N.)

'65 MUSTANG COUPE. This rear view of a '65 Mustang shows the center-rear fuel filler, a carryover from Falcon. This could lead to awkward fueling, requiring two hands, one to hold open the spring-loaded gas cap and the other to hold the fuel nozzle. The Mustang coupe was credited with 8.8 cubic feet of "usable luggage capacity" in the trunk, but the convertible trunk was so much smaller that in Mustang's advance press information kit, Ford listed it as "N.A." (not available). Presumably, for the nearly 102,000 customers who bought first-year Mustang convertibles, trunk space was not an issue. (N.)

'66 MUSTANG AND ELECTRIC VEHICLE. Ford Motor Company shipped demonstration models of Mustang to its European companies. In the United Kingdom, its local publicists photographed this '66 in tandem with an experimental battery-electric "city car." For the first time, the 2015 50th Anniversary Mustang will be manufactured (at Ford's Flat Rock plant near Detroit) with right-hand drive (RHD) for such overseas markets as UK, Australia, Japan, and other RHD countries, mostly former British colonies. (N.)

'65 2+2. Ford added a third body type to its mix of 1965 Mustangs late in the model year, the "2+2" or fastback. Production of the fastback version commenced on August 17, 1964, although the 1965 model year did not officially begin until October 1, 1964. Other late changes to the Mustang included substitution of a 200-cid Six for the 170, and availability of the high-performance 289 V-8. These "running" changes in the product have created some confusion and dispute among Mustang fans, who persist in delineating early Mustangs as "64 1/2" year models, although all first-year Mustangs are, according to their VINs, 1965 models. (N.)

2+2 AT NEW YORK WORLD'S FAIR. Late in the summer of 1964, with production of the fastback in sight or already started, perhaps even before formal dealer showroom sales were permitted, Ford put versions of the new body style on display inside its New York World's Fair pavilion. The above photograph shows a version with a racing-type paint job, including a blue stripe from front to rear. The below photograph shows another Mustang fastback, displayed outside the pavilion. Local publicity would have drawn metro New York visitors, and wire services and New York–based national media reached out to people farther away with possible New York visit plans. (Both, FC.)

'66 MUSTANG WITH TAPE PLAYER. In an odd way, the otherwise little-changed 1966 Mustang debuted what may have been one of the first electronic introductions to the international automotive industry: the eight-track tape player. This new option, shown here, was aimed at enhancing entertainment rather than vehicle performance, safety, or pollution control. This photograph also shows Mustang's new-for-1966 instrument cluster. Note the round dials, in comparison to the '65 Mustang cluster (see pages 52, 53, 57, and 59). Eight-track tapes provided hours of uninterrupted music to ease long-distance travel by car. Later, cassette tapes performed that task and, today, the mediums are compact discs, MP3 players, and satellite radio. Audio systems are today a major issue for option lists. In 1964, automobiles were merely advancing from the AM-radio universe. (N.)

'66 CONVERTIBLE. Superficially, the 1966 Mustang (available October 1, 1965) was little changed from the original introduced a year and a half earlier. It offered exterior trim changes (including new-appearance wheel covers), different engine choices, and a new instrument panel. The new model continued to sell uninterruptedly at a record pace. (N.)

'66 MUSTANG. This photograph shows the front styling of the base 1966 Mustang. The racing horse emblem in the grille continues, but the vertical and horizontal bars in the grille are gone. (N.)

'66 MUSTANG GT. For 1966, the Mustang GT series took on a distinct identity, with a pair of driving lights located within the grille to augment driver vision at night, connected stylistically by a horizontal bar. Mustangs achieved a record output of 607,568 units in 1966 for the three body styles, including some 253,000 Sixes and 354,000 V-8s. (N.)

'66 GT, REAR VIEW. This photograph reveals the unique dual exhausts of the GT model. These duals are connected to the standard V-8 engine in the GT and provide for higher performance, through reduced back pressure, compared to Mustangs with single exhausts. (N.)

'66 INSTRUMENT PANEL. The distinctive instrument panel of the 1966 Mustang featured wood-grain panels on both sides beneath the protective pad across the top, and round dials. In this version, the car is equipped with the floor-mounted automatic transmission control. (N.)

'66 WHEEL COVERS. Another sign for identifying a 1966 model Mustang, compared to a 1965, are the distinctive wheel covers, as shown here. This photograph also shows where the Mustang badge on the front quarter panel was mounted. For cars with a V-8, a 289 medallion would be mounted forward of the front wheel cut. (N.)

ONE-MILLIONTH MUSTANG. Prior to its April 17 second anniversary, in the midst of the 1966 model year, Ford was able to claim that Mustang had achieved a record one-million production mark, easily passing the previous record by Falcon in 1960. To promote the news, Ford Division arranged to have an aerial photograph taken of 55 Mustangs carefully parked outside its headquarters, spelling out "1,000,000." Before its introduction, annual volume estimates were as low as 80,000. By selling 418,812 units in the 1965 model year, Mustang became the most successful new car in automotive history, surpassing the previous record by the 1960 Falcon. (N.)

Six

PONY CARS AND MUSCLE CARS
1964–1974

'65 MUSTANG "SPECIAL." An overt example of "pony car" Mustang also entering the muscle car field was recognition of a modified 1966 fastback for its performance potential. Here, Ford Division general manager Dr. Donald N. Frey (left) accepts the America's Perfect Performance Car award from Bob Tasca, a Rhode Island Ford dealer active in promoting performance events. The date is September 23, 1965, just before the 1966 model introduction on October 1. (N.)

'64 PONTIAC GTO. Automobile enthusiasts generally credit Pontiac's 1964 GTO model (shown here) as being the first muscle car. Based on a midsized Le Mans coupe, GTOs (called "Goats" by fans) featured a larger V-8—up to 421-cid and 350-horsepower from full-sized Pontiacs, plus some tweaking—in place of the tepid six-cylinder, 140-horsepower motor standard in the Le Mans. Pontiac also named its various models for global performance events or custom-built race cars. (N.)

'65 PLYMOUTH BARRACUDA. Chrysler Corporation got a two-week jump on Ford by introducing its fastback Barracuda (shown here in a reference photograph) on April 1, 1964, though sales did not commence until May. Barracuda was derived from the compact Valiant sedan. But Barracuda did not enjoy the public notice accorded Mustang among the "pony car" audience. Some years later, the Barracuda morphed into a high-performance model called "Cuda" (see page 84). (N.)

'65 Plymouth Rally Car. Plymouth elected to approach performance events gently, as with this Plymouth Barracuda Rally model. Meanwhile, for the 1963 model year, the Valiant line had been expanded to include hardtop coupes and convertibles. Rally events in the United States at the time were considered more respectable than closed-track oval racing and straight-line drag racing. (N.)

'66 AMC Marlin. As Mustang and Pontiac successes quickly became widely known, and dealers demanded vehicles of their own brands to compete, the pony and muscle market niches were filled by all the major players in the US automobile market. Shown here is the American Motors entry, a midsized fastback 1965 Rambler Marlin, introduced in February 1965. Its base engine was a 232-cid Six with optional 287-cid and 327-cid V-8s. Production for 1965 was a modest 10,327. (N.)

'66 DODGE CHARGER. Dodge, Plymouth's brother division at Chrysler, responded to the muscle car market with this Charger model for 1966, based on the midsized Coronet 500 series. The fastback design made it recognizable as a muscle car. Some 37,300 Chargers were produced for 1966, with an engine range from a 225-cid Six to V-8s up to 273-cid. (N.)

'67 MUSTANGS. Still sharing key mechanicals with other Ford models, the 1967 Mustang was enlarged in the front end to accommodate the bigger FE series V-8 engines, specifically the 315-horsepower, 390-cid GT version offered on the intermediate Fairlane the previous year. Overall length increased two inches, the body was wider, and there was a weight gain of 129 pounds in the base model coupe. Shown here are all three '67 Mustang body styles. (N.)

'67 MUSTANG GT. Here, a 1967 Mustang GT model is shown airborne on a Ford test track during its developmental prove-out with the heavier, more powerful 390-cid engine and other changes from the Mustang of 1964. There was now a separate identity (GT) for the designated high-performance Mustang model, with vehicle design of signature twin road lights positioned in the grille, and ribbon, or banner, decals horizontally located from the front to the rear wheel cutouts across the lower part of the doors. (N.)

'67 MERCURY COUGAR EMBLEM. For 1967, Ford Division's internal competitor, Lincoln-Mercury, brought out its own Mustang-based sporty coupe, an upscale "pony" named Cougar with a 111-inch wheelbase—two and a half inches more than Mustang. Shown here is the Cougar emblem mounted in the grille, conceptually similar to Mustang's running horse. As with Mustang, Cougar's inner-body panels were shared with other Ford and Mercury compact and midsized cars, but outer panels were unique, providing distinction. Cougars were initially offered with only a single body style, the two-door hardtop coupe, and engine choices were exclusively V-8s. (N.)

'67 MERCURY COUGAR. This is the Cougar production car. Cougars came with a choice of three V-8 engines and a host of luxury options standard. Quad headlamps, concealed behind doors, automatically opened when the lights were illuminated. At the rear, horizontal groups of three lamps on each side behind a corner-to-corner strip presented sequential taillights, an upscale feature pioneered by Ford Thunderbirds. (N.)

'67 CHEVROLET CAMARO Z28. This shows the rear view of a 1967 Chevrolet Camaro Z28, a performance coupe that was Chevy's muscle car response to rival Mustang over two years after the Mustang introduction. At the beginning, Chevrolet (and Pontiac) seemed to emphasize performance more than Ford did, although much of the high-speed marketing was carried out away from the mainstream of the public to avoid media and Washington criticism. (N.)

'67 CHEVROLET NOVA SS. Ford's archrival for decades was Chevrolet, with competition felt at both dealers and respective metro Detroit offices. Chevy initially confined its performance cars to Corvette and full-sized Chevys. Mustang changed Chevrolet's orientation, resulting in the 1967 Camaro and a broader offering of other "hot" cars. This is the once family-friendly Falcon-fighter, a '67 Chevy II Nova Super Sport model with racing symbol badges, now offered with a 275-horsepower V-8. (N.)

'68 CHEVROLET CAMARO. This is the standard 1968 Camaro, little changed from the '67. Camaro quickly became the most significant of the non-Ford pony cars. Ford, with its "Six and the Single Girl" television advertisements, and Chevrolet, which always aimed at being the auto market's value buy, did well with women customers. Camaro was only slightly different from Mustang in price, weight, and engine options. (N.)

'67 Pontiac Firebird. A second pony car selling against Mustang and Cougar in 1967 was the Pontiac Firebird, built on the same platform as the Chevrolet Camaro, with dimensions largely matching those of Mustang. Since Pontiac had founded the muscle car market with the GTO three years earlier, Firebird was unquestionably the company's pony car. It was introduced in January 1967 with an array of engines, including two Sixes and three V-8s. (N.)

'67 Mustang GT Fastback. By the time the 1967 Mustangs were introduced on September 30, 1966, Ford had concluded that the pony Mustang had morphed into a muscle car Mustang, thanks to the GT (for Gran Turismo, an Italian road-racing classification). The car had an optional 390-cid V-8. Production of '67s reached 472,121 for the year. (N.)

'68 MUSTANGS. Here, a team of two 1968 Mustang GTs are shown in their quest for a third consecutive Sports Car Club of America Trans-American Championship for sedans. A similar "muscular" 1968 Mustang starred in the movie *Bullitt* in a four-minute chase scene. Production of the 1968 model year Mustang exceeded 317,000. (N.)

'68 SHELBY GT500. In midyear 1968, Ford concluded an agreement with sportsman and independent racing car builder Carroll Shelby, the result being the GT500 Shelby Cobra, sold by selected Ford dealers. This front view of a Cobra coupe shows its unique hood louvers, rear quarter scoops, and grille modifications. The Cobra sold in limited volume and at a premium price. (N.)

'68 SHELBY GT500 CONVERTIBLE. This rear view of the Shelby Cobra shows its spoiler, taillights, and heavy-duty tires. Cobra went on to be attached to high-performance Mustang and other Ford models, and the relationship between Shelby and Ford waxed and waned over the years. (N.)

'68 MUSTANG COBRA JET. Ford's own mid-model-year Mustang Cobra Jet is seen here with racing stripe, blanked rear-quarter windows, and racing tires. Cobra Jet was actually the name of the 428-cid V-8 of Ford's FE V-8 engine family, introduced in April 1968 for the performance market. The name was used in subsequent model years for several limited-production engines (335/385/429) aimed at the same market. (N.)

76

'69 MUSTANG GRANDE. Meanwhile, Mustang was used as a platform for the pony car "luxury" market with this 1969 Grande, offered in only the coupe body, priced at $2,954 (as compared to $2,618 for the base Mustang coupe). Note the Grande's standard vinyl roof. Vinyl roofs were popular and profitable options for Ford in this era. Though Mustang sales and production lagged, it remained a surprisingly large-volume car for Ford: 300,000 for 1969. (N.)

'69 FORD OF EUROPE CAPRI. For 1969, Ford entered a third model in the pony car market: this European Ford Capri coupe, sold in North America by Lincoln-Mercury dealers. The left-hand drive car shown here is Belgium or German built. Note the European-style headlamps. Over a five-year period, it was very popular among Europeans, toting up sales of 1,169,088. Initially, Capri came with only a 1.6-liter Four. Added later were 2.0-liter and 2.3-liter Fours and a 2.6-liter V-6. Only the coupe body was offered. (N.)

'69 Dodge Dart Swinger and R/T. For the 1969 and 1970 model years, Chrysler unleashed a platoon of pony and muscle cars, including the compact Dodge Dart Swinger (above), intermediate-sized Dodge Super Bee and R/T models (below), and the Plymouth intermediate-sized Road Runner, all with engine sizes up to 340-cid and 383-cid. The cars were designed to be raced and had graphic appliques of bees and the Road Runner cartoon character. (N.)

'70 Dodge Challenger. A new entry in the Dodge pony/muscle car market was the Challenger (shown here). Based on the Dart compact, with a 111-inch wheelbase, it offered an array of engine choices and three body styles: convertible and two different two-door coupes. This car was positioned against the Mustang and Camaro. Prices ranged from $2,851 for the base coupe to $3,198 for the convertible. The R/T was the high-performance version. (N.)

'70 Dodge Upscale Challenger. Dodge matched Mustang's move to the luxury or upscale end of the pony/muscle car niche. This is the midsized 1970 Dodge Challenger "Special Edition." More creature comforts were included in this car's package than were offered in the performance version of the car. (N.)

'70 FORD TORINO GT. Ford's Torino was the top series of the once family-car intermediate Fairlane label, pioneered as a midsized model in 1962. For 1969, it took a turn to muscle cars with the Torino GT series. Fastback Torino GTs were priced at $3,270 for the Cobra version with 250-horsepower, 351-cid V-8, versus the same body Torino Six at $2,610. A '70 Model Torino GT is pictured here. The wheelbase was 114 inches. (N.)

'69 MUSTANG BOSS 429. Ford Division also expanded the Mustang brand as a muscle car for 1969, introducing this Boss 429 model. Another was the high-performance Mach I, an exaggerated fastback (like the Torino) priced at $3,122, with the 351-cid V-8 standard and 390- and 428-cid Cobra Jet V-8s optional. Model-year production for Mustang stayed steady, at just under 300,000. All '69 Mustangs had substantial appearance changes from previous models, supporting quad headlights. (N.)

'70 BOSS 302 MUSTANG. In the summer of 2012, at a regional meeting of the Shelby American Automobile Club (SAAC), unusual photographic pairings of two very different Mustangs took place. Club members with Mustangs were able to have them pictured with another type of racer, the World War II North American Aviation P-51 Mustang fighter, popular at air races. The $3,720 1969–1970 Boss 302 Mustang shown here was eligible to compete in SCCA Trans-Am road races. (N.)

'71 DATSUN 240Z. The Datsun 240Z shown here was much in the Mustang tradition in terms of appearance: fastback coupe with long hood and performance to match. Datsun later changed its name for the North American market to Nissan. The 240Z was relatively popular. Sales for 1970 came to 16,000, jumping to nearly 34,000 for 1971. The import's wheelbase was 91 inches, and it was priced at $3,528 with a 2.4-liter, 151-horepower overhead cam Six. (N.)

'71 Ford Mavericks. Ford introduced new nameplates for 1970 in a midyear 1969 announcement: the $1,995 Maverick, plus a sister car for Lincoln-Mercury, continuing the Comet name. The following year, Maverick offered the Grabber performance model, shown here at upper left, featuring racing stripes and an optional 302-cid V-8. The 1971 Maverick Grabbers were priced at $2,523. Maverick output was 451,000 for the new 1970 model, dropping to 272,000 for the '71. (N.)

'71 Mustang Sportsroof. Mustangs were completely restyled for 1971—longer and heavier, including weight gains from mandatory federal safety and emission regulations. Prices ranged from $2,911 to $3,220 without extra cost options. Production had fallen off from the halcyon days of 1964–1966, declining from 300,000 in 1969 to 190,000 in 1970 and 150,000 for 1971. As shown in this chapter, there were now many more competitors in the pony and muscle niche markets. (N.)

'71 MUSTANG MACH I. The above photograph shows the front of the '71 Mustang Mach I model, with running lights within the grille and hood scoops. These features were not to be found on regular Mustangs. Below is the '71 instrument panel, quite different from those in earlier model year Mustangs. In effect, Ford was producing two distinct Mustangs: a base model that still could be considered a pony car; and the Mach 1, definitely a muscle car. (N.)

'72 CUDA AND '74 ROAD RUNNER. Mustang's competitors kept pouring on the coal as the 1970s progressed, offering both pony cars and muscle cars. Shown here are two from Chrysler: a $2,953 "Pony" '72 Plymouth Cuda (above) on a 108-inch wheelbase, based on the compact Valiant; and a midsized $3,545 Plymouth Road Runner (below) with a 115-inch wheelbase. Cartoon Road Runner appliques were applied on the C-pillars behind the rear quarter windows. (N.)

'73 GRAND AM AND '74 TRANS AM FIREBIRD. Here are Pontiac's offerings for the pony car and muscle car markets in the early 1970s: the midsized $3,992 '73 Grand Am (above) on a 112-inch wheelbase; and the $4,446 Pony '74 Firebird (below) on a 108-inch wheelbase with large decal on the hood. The Firebird Trans Am was further popularized by its role in a 1977 cross-country chase movie, *Smokey and the Bandit.* One of Mustang's toughest competitors was the Firebird, especially after the 1974 model shown here, with its huge graphic of the mythical southwestern desert bird popularized by Native Americans. Mustang and other 1970s cars adopted the fad of large emblem appliques. Though lionized in enthusiast magazines, sales—and, thus, production—of the two performance Pontiacs were modest: 43,100 for the '73 Grand Am and 73,700 for the total of four 1974 Firebird variations. (Above, N; below, G.)

'72 MUSTANG. This photograph of a 1972 Mustang coupe shows a Grande series complete with vinyl top and color-coordinated outside mirrors and wheel covers. Mustang overall length had grown to 190 inches, 10 more than the first Mustangs of 1964–1966, with attendant weight gain. Federal safety, bumper, and exhaust regulations contributed to size and weight gains. (N.)

'73 MUSTANG CONVERTIBLE. The Mustang shown here was Ford's only convertible model that year and, significantly, the last Ford convertible for 10 years. Convertibles were criticized as unsafe in rollover crashes and had grown out of favor with the buying public because of advances in air-conditioning. In addition, interstate highways allowed faster travel, which in turn made "top down" motoring unpleasant at higher speeds. In addition, top-down driving invited roadway grit. (N.)

Seven

GENERATION TWO
PINTO-BASED MUSTANG II
1974–1978

'74 PINTO HATCHBACK. Reacting to the continued popularity of imported subcompact cars, Ford and Chevrolet each introduced their own subcompact four-cylinder models for 1971, the Ford Pinto and Chevrolet Vega. Ford used the platform of its Pinto to create the pint-sized Mustang II. (N.)

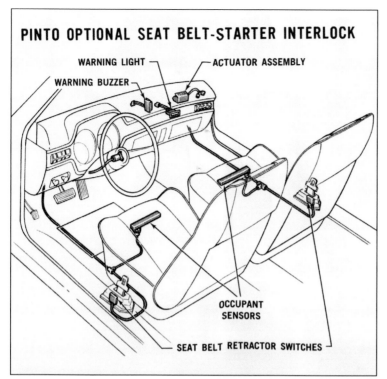

PINTO OPTIONAL SEAT BELT-STARTER INTERLOCK

WARNING LIGHT
ACTUATOR ASSEMBLY
WARNING BUZZER
OCCUPANT SENSORS
SEAT BELT RETRACTOR SWITCHES

IGNITION INTERLOCK. This diagram shows the relative complexity of the government-mandated seat belt interlock, which prevented a car (here, a Pinto) being started unless seat belts were fastened. The public complained to Congress, which quickly withdrew the regulation midway in the 1974 model year. That year's models of all makes also were unfavorably affected by new regulations calling for five-mile-per-hour-impact, damage-free front and rear bumpers. (N.)

'74 CHEVROLET Z28. While Ford was pulling back on its muscle cars for 1974 with the Pinto-based Mustang II, rival Chevrolet was pushing forward. Shown here is the high-performance '74 Chevy Z28 version of the Camaro model most closely matched against Mustangs in prior years. The Z28 variation was mainly trim (including front and rear "spoilers" for race-track speed) and standard V-8 engines of 350 and 400 cid and 160 and 185 horsepower, respectively. (N.)

IACOCCA WITH '65 AND '74 MUSTANGS. The downsized Mustang II of 1974 was, like the original 'Stang of 1964, very much an Iacocca car. The initial publicity photograph, shown here, featured Iacocca in front of a white Mustang II notchback coupe with a similar 1965 Mustang in the background for comparison. Ford produced nearly 386,000 Mustang IIs in 1974, while Chevrolet made 146,600 Camaros. Pinto production for 1974 amounted to 544,200. Pinto prices had risen to $2,527 by 1974, up from $1,919 at its 1971 introduction. Mustang II prices for 1974 started at $3,081. (FT.)

'74 MUSTANG COUPE AND MACH I FASTBACK. There were three body styles of the four-place Mustang II: a notchback coupe (above), a three-door hatchback, and a fastback coupe (below). As previously noted, there was no convertible model, as in past Mustangs. With an overall length of 175 inches, Mustang II was seven inches shorter than the original 1965 model and 13 inches less than the 1973 model. Mustang II's 96.2-inch wheelbase was nearly a foot shorter than the first Mustang. For the notchback coupe, Ford played up the input of its recently acquired Ghia studio in Italy, emphasizing luxury rather than high-speed performance. (Both, N.)

"MPG" Model Assembly. International turmoil in the fall of 1973, especially in the Middle East, resulted in an embargo on shipping oil from the region to Europe and North America. In early 1974, this in turn led to huge increases in gasoline prices and spot shortages. Motorists were afraid they would be unable to buy fuel for their vehicles. Ford responded by re-engineering some cars for markedly better fuel economy. Here, a 1975 Mustang II "MPG" model is shown at Dearborn Assembly Plant. The MPG model featured changes in gear and rear-axle ratios to maximize highway fuel economy, at the expense of good drivability, especially on manual-transmission cars. (N.)

2.3-LITER ENGINE. The base engine in Mustang II was this 92-horsepower overhead cam, 2.3-liter (140-cid) Four, the first Ford US-built engine in metric measures. It was augmented by an optional 103-horsepower, 2.8-liter V-6 engine imported from Ford of Germany and, beginning with 1975 models, Ford's well-proven 5.0-liter (302-cid) V-8 rated at 134 horsepower. This 2.3 was commonly called the Lima engine, for the city in Ohio where it was built, to distinguish it from 2.3s built elsewhere. (N.)

'78 COBRA II. In its five-year run, Mustang II had only negligible appearance changes, mainly consisting of new tape and paint treatments and modified wheel covers and other trim. A series of high-performance models beginning with the 1976 Stallion were mainly distinguished by superficial changes, including added front and rear spoilers. The paint-and-tape treatment is applied to this 1978 Mustang II Cobra. There also was a King Cobra model. (N.)

Eight

GENERATION THREE FOX MUSTANGS 1979–1993

'78 "FOX" FAIRMONT FUTURA. For model year 1978, Ford unveiled a new family of compact cars: the Fairmont and its sister, the Mercury Zephyr. Fairmont, a replacement for the Falcon/Comet of 1960, also was to provide a platform for the next-generation 1979 Mustang. Fairmont cars were offered in four body styles: two- and four-door sedans, four-door station wagon, and the Ford Futura sporty coupe shown here. The new family of Ford Motor Company cars was known informally as "Fox" cars, derived from the code name for the platform. Ford described the Futura as a "personal specialty car." (N.)

'79 MUSTANG TEASER. Weeks, if not months, before the October 5, 1978, dealer introduction of the "all-new" 1979 Mustang, Ford Division Public Relations issued this teaser photograph to the media. This was a direct teaser, in contrast to the various full-scale show or dream cars publicized before the 1964 introduction of the original Mustang. Showing only a few inches of the 1979 car's front end, with a drawing in the background, the teaser played the role that new cars under shrouds and dealerships' opaque showroom windows used to play in the buildup to Intro Day. (N.)

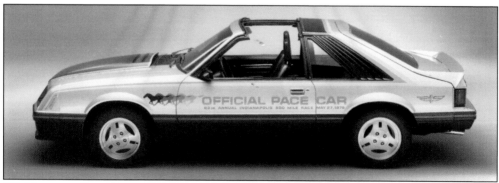

'79 MUSTANG INDY PACE CAR. Repeating elements of the 1965 Mustang introduction, Ford wangled the honorary "pace car" designation for the 1979 T-Top Mustang (shown here). It was the first time since 1964 that Mustang had been so honored. Some 6,000 Mustang Pace Car Replicas were built for sale. Engine choices included the base 2.3-liter Four, a turbocharged 2.3 Four, a 2.8-liter V-6, and a 5.0-liter V-8. (N.)

'79 MERCURY CAPRI. The 1979 Mercury Capri, marketed by Lincoln-Mercury dealers, was mechanically similar to the '79 Mustang, except for its distinctive grille and side and rear sheet-metal panels. But it was built in only one body style, the three-door hatch/fastback. The Capri name previously was used for a Ford of Europe pony car popular in the UK and on the continent and imported for Mercury dealers to sell in North America. Shown here is the "sporty" RS series '79 Capri. (N.)

'79 MEGASTAR. At both major and regional auto shows, usually sponsored by local dealers to attract prospects, it was desirable to "reveal" a show or dream car, such as this Ford Megastar II. Creating such vehicles may or may not reveal future styling trends, but they have always been crowd pleasers. And consumer feedback provides an automotive company important information about whether the design elements should be developed in future production vehicles. (N.)

'79 MUSTANG AND LTD. After a long dry period of new Ford products, 1979 was a major year for introduction of new models: Ford Mustang (foreground), Mercury Capri, Grand Marquis, and Ford LTD (rear). The Marquis and the LTD were built on Ford's new "Panther" body-and-frame, rear-drive platform, applied to Lincoln and Continental the following year. The Panther platform characterized Ford's large cars through the end of the 2011 model run. One adverse result of the many "all-new" platforms in 1978–1980 was the lack of appearance changes on these cars during the 1980s. However, Ford used the funds thus freed to introduce several other all-new vehicles in the decade. (N.)

'81 Mercury Capri T-Top. In place of the convertibles missing from Ford Motor Company sporty cars (and competitors) after 1972, a new fresh-air option became available: the removable T-Top. This 1981 Mercury Capri is equipped with a T-Top. The same was available for Mustang. The T-Top option cost an extra $874 above the Capri three-door's base $6,685 and the base Mustang three-door at $6,408. Generally, there were few appearance changes for either 1980 or 1981 models of Mustang and Capri. (N.)

'82 Ford Escort. Ford Motor Company's major focus for 1980–1982 was on the new Panther-platform Lincoln and Continental and, at the other end of the spectrum, a new subcompact family, the Ford Escort (shown here in its three body styles). These cars were intended for Ford dealers; the companion Mercury Lynx was sold by Lincoln-Mercury. Prices for the 94.2-inch-wheelbase '82 Escort, Ford's first North American front-wheel-drive subcompact and smallest engine (65 horsepower, 1.6 liter), started at $5,158. (N.)

'82 MUSTANG GT.
According to a plan well established by 1982, there were two separate front-end appearances for Mustang, illustrated by this GT series model with front spoiler and air dam and running lights beneath the grille. For the first time since 1979 models, the "Boss" 302-cid V-8 was optional. Fox Mustangs continued at an overall length of 179 inches on a 100.4-inch wheelbase, and the base price was $6,345 ($8,308 for the GT shown here). (N.)

'55 T-BIRD VS. '82 EXP.
Ford's product portfolio expanded again for 1982, with the two-place Ford EXP and Mercury LN7, based on the prior year's Escort/Lynx. Ford marketers issued this comparison illustration of the EXP and the 1955 Thunderbird, the company's previous two-place car. The two front-drive subcompacts likely cut into the Mustang's once strong position as a pony car, but helped the company's Corporate Average Fuel Economy score, mandated by Congress. (N.)

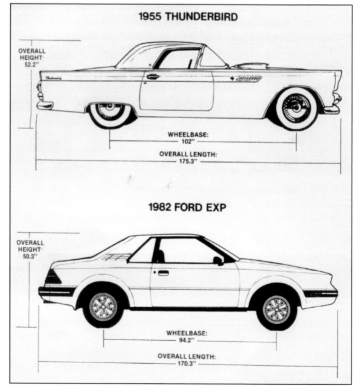

1955 THUNDERBIRD

OVERALL HEIGHT: 52.2"

WHEELBASE: 102"

OVERALL LENGTH: 175.3"

1982 FORD EXP

OVERALL HEIGHT: 50.3"

WHEELBASE: 94.2"

OVERALL LENGTH: 170.3"

'83 CAPRI BUBBLEBACK AND '83 MUSTANG CONVERTIBLE. Ford was inching back to convertibles, first with the T-Top, then with an exclusive-for-Capri "bubbleback" curved, molded glass backlite (above). Police agencies began buying 5.0-liter Mustangs to use as pursuit vehicles. A month after introduction of other 1983 models, Ford unveiled its first convertible since the 1973 model, the 1983 Mustang (below). Mustang convertibles started as coupes at Ford's Rouge (Dearborn Assembly) Plant and were transported to an off-site vendor, where the steel roof was removed and convertible top and related hardware installed. Mercury did not offer a similar convertible. At $9,449, the 1983 Mustang convertible was the brand's costliest product. Capri and Mustang both offered a new 3.8-liter V-6 engine in place of the old inline Six dating back to the Falcon days. (N.)

'83 FORD MODELS. Shown here in one photograph are each of Ford Motor Company's all-new North American cars and light trucks for the 1983 model year. Those shown include, from front to rear, Thunderbird, Cougar, bubbleback Capri, Mustang convertible, downsized LTD, Ranger small pickup, Escort hatchback four-door sedan, downsized Marquis, Escort GT, compact Topaz, compact Tempo, and small 4WD Bronco II. When the original Mustang was introduced in 1964, the company (and its competitors) offered far fewer sizes and makes, but a greater variety of body types. (N.)

'84 MUSTANG TURBO GT CONVERTIBLE. The 1984 Turbo GT Mustang convertible was a relatively rare Mustang, with total production less than 650 cars. The car pictured here was the author's personal car for 10 years and has been in the family for over 25 years. Both handling and fuel economy are outstanding. The below photograph shows the '84 Mustang's interior, with gray vinyl upholstery to match the exterior's red and black colors. Because of its durability, vinyl was a favored automotive trim material beginning in the mid-1950s. It began to lose favor to leather in the 1970s, due to vinyl's base chemical composition, derived from petroleum. (Both, D.)

'84 MUSTANG SVO COUPE. To develop limited-production, high-performance models, especially for sanctioned racing, Ford organized a Special Vehicles Operation (SVO). The SVO team tweaked the turbo-charged, 2.3-liter Four, similar to that in the T-Bird and Mustang Turbo GT regular production cars, to match the front-end appearance of SVO Mustangs, such as the 1984 model shown here. Note the fresh-air hood scoop and absence of grille. (N.)

'85 MUSTANG GT. For the 1985 GT model, Mustang's front styling was influenced by the prior year's SVO, with open slots in favor of crosshatch grille. Higher-horsepower engine choices suggest the Mustang had almost completely morphed into a muscle car, but economical choices of four-cylinder engine and manual transmission left the choice to the buyer. (N.)

'85 Mustang SVO. All SVO Mustangs were produced as the three-door hatchback. Production of 1985 Mustangs came to 84,600 hatchbacks (SVO included), 56,800 notchback coupes and 15,100 convertibles. Model-year production included 80,000 Fours, 18,000 Sixes, and 45,000 V-8s. The SVO was premium priced at $14,521, while the base Four-cylinder coupe went for $6,885. (N.)

'87 Mustang and '51 Ford. Shown here are two Fords, side by side but 36 years apart: a 1951 Ford (left) and a 1987 Mustang, pictured at the Jack Roush collection in Livonia, Michigan. The '51 appears to be a $1,925 Victoria, Ford's first pillarless hardtop, on a 114-inch wheelbase with overall length of 196.4. The $8,474 hatchback '87 Mustang rests on a 100.5-inch wheelbase with overall length of 179.6. There were only two engine choices in 1951, a 101-horsepower Six and a 110-horsepower V-8, and there were no other US Ford-brand cars to choose from. (D.)

MUSTANG'S 25TH ANNIVERSARY. The year 1989 marked Mustang's 25th anniversary, but festivities were limited by the prospect of the car being replaced by the Japanese-based Probe (opposite page). This publicity photograph shows the '89 Mustang (foreground) with an original '65. However, Mustang sales continued strong even in the face of internal competition from Probe. The customers were overthrowing the auto company managers. (N.)

'89 PROBE. In the mid-1980s, Ford management decided that the Mustang had run its course and needed to be replaced. Accordingly, an arrangement was made between Ford and Mazda Motors of Japan (in which Ford had a large investment) to replace rear-drive Mustang with a "modern" front-wheel-drive car named Probe, to be built at a Mazda/Ford assembly plant near Detroit. The base-priced $10,459 Probe was introduced on May 12, 1988, as a pull-ahead 1989 model. The car, 177 inches long on a 99-inch wheelbase, had a Mazda 2.2-liter, four-cylinder engine. (N.)

'90 MUSTANG, FRONT. For its 1990 model, a small grille was restored to the Mustang's front appearance, as shown here. The auto market was weak in 1990, with industry sales declining each year since 1988. The slump was to last several years. In its 26th year, Mustang production slipped to a still-respectable 128,200, but there would be further dips ahead. Nevertheless, the big change for the 1994 model Mustang was already programmed. (N.)

'90 MUSTANG, REAR. Shown here is a rear view of the 1990 Mustang. In the great tradition of American cars up to this time, there was a long list of additional cost options available for Mustang. Imported cars offered few options because of long shipping times from overseas, whereas American manufacturers felt customers wanted to be able to customize their new cars by choosing from the option list. (N.)

'91 PROBE. Restoring grilles to the front ends of Ford products seemed to be in fashion in 1990. Here is the Probe showing off its latticework. The rear appearance also was changed. The main news was the availability of a 3.0-liter, 140-horsepower V-6. The base price of $11,691 was $1,232 higher than for the introductory 1989 Probe. (N.)

'92 MUSTANG 5.0. The final years of the Fox-based Mustang brought few appearance and equipment changes. This photograph shows the rear quarter of a 1992 Mustang convertible. The following year's Mustang was to be the last year for the Fox-based Mustang, introduced for 1979. A 14-year run of a car's chassis was unusually long for an American car, where competition and dealer demands call for frequent updating. (N.)

'93 MUSTANG GT. The last year of the Fox Mustang generation was presented in three series, a limited edition Cobra, a V-8 GT (shown), and a base LX in three bodies, the $10,719 base coupe, $11,244 hatchback (or three-door), and the company's only North American convertible at $17,548. All prices were for the venerable 2.3-liter 105-horsepower Four, now in its final year in Mustang. Production totaled 114,400 for the model year. (N.)

'93 CAMARO. Mustang's main rival, the Chevrolet Camaro, was totally redesigned for 1993, its fourth generation and a year ahead of an all-new Mustang. For 1993, Camaro offered only one body style, a $13,339 coupe. A high-performance $16,799 Z-28 with a 275-horsepower Corvette engine was the Indy pace car. But Camaro production reached only 39,100. (N.)

EMPLOYEE CAR SHOW. Coming up on Mustang's 30th anniversary with an all-new generation on tap, a Mustang employee car show was held at the Ford Research and Engineering Center (shown here) to introduce the 1994 fourth generation to employees. The first public showing was at the Detroit Auto Show in January 1993. (N.)

Nine

GENERATION FOUR NEW EDGE MUSTANGS 1994–2004

'94 MUSTANG CUTAWAY. This phantom, or cutaway, view of the first all-new Mustang in 15 years was issued to automotive enthusiast and trade magazines, more because it was expected (and thus demanded) than because it supplied useful information. In addition to total restyling to present a streamlined, rounded appearance—called "jellybean" and earlier seen in Ford Thunderbird and Taurus—the '94 Mustang offered new marketing series but only two body styles, coupe and convertible. The base engine, no longer a Four, was replaced by a 3.8-liter V-6, an engine also used in the Ford Taurus, Mercury Sable, and Lincoln Continental. (N.)

'94 MUSTANG BASE CONVERTIBLE. The base '94 Mustang coupe with the 145-horsepower V-6 was priced at $13,355 and weighed 3,055 pounds. The similarly equipped convertible was $20,150. Convertible production for the year came to a surprising 44,700, compared to 78,500 for the coupe. Only 6,009 of the 1994 Cobra, basically a race car, were produced. The new model's footprint was virtually the same as its predecessor: 101-inch wheelbase, with overall length of 181.5 and width of 71.8 inches. (N.)

'94 MUSTANG INSTRUMENT PANEL. This photograph shows the 1994 Mustang cockpit. For the first time in a Mustang, safety air bags to cushion front-seat occupants in frontal collisions were standard: one in the steering-wheel hub and the other on the right side of the instrument panel. The instrument panel bears little resemblance to the "dual cowl" design of earlier Mustang models. (N.)

'94 MUSTANG GT. The distinctive appearance of the '94 Mustang GT series from base cars is difficult to discern in this photograph. Aside from identifying badges, the GT has larger diameter wheels and different wheel designs. Less visible is its standard V-8 engine with twin tailpipes. The standard engine for 1994 and 1995 GTs was the familiar 302-cid (5.0-liter) V-8 with 215 horsepower. Transmissions were a five-speed manual and an optional four-speed-overdrive automatic. (N.)

'94 INDY COBRA. For the third time in its history, Mustang was the Indy 500 pace car in 1994. The Cobra convertible is shown here with its predecessor Mustang open-air 1965 convertible and 1979 T-roof pace cars. Visible in the foreground is the original brick track surface. Only 1,000 of the 1994 Cobra convertibles were built, priced at $23,535. The Cobra engine was a special 302-V-8 that produced 340 horsepower. The wheels, 17 inches in diameter, were an inch larger than those on a GT, and two inches larger than on the base Mustang. (N.)

'95 MUSTANG SVT COBRA. In its 1995 models, the only easily visible difference between the 1994 and the $24,070 1995 SVT Cobra (shown here) was in its wheels, compared with the '94 Cobra pictured on the previous page as an Indianapolis 500 pace car. Even with little change, though, Mustang continued to sell relatively well: coupe production was 120,400, and convertibles, 44,600. This year only, a GTS coupe series was offered with the base V-8 with a price tag of $16,910, exactly $995 less than the GT coupe. SVT Cobras for 1999 featured independent rear suspension. (N.)

'96 MUSTANG GT. For 1996 Mustangs, the changes—at least for the V-8 options—again were less seen than felt. Ford's "small block" 302 V-8, in use for 30 years, was retired in favor of a new, "modular" 4.6-liter (281-cid) single overhead cam 215-horsepower motor, standard in GT (shown here) and Cobra models. The GT was distinguished from base Mustangs by its rear spoiler on the deck lid and dual exhausts; Cobra was notable for air-intake scoops in the hood. Production for the year fell to 92,600 coupes and 33,800 convertibles. (N.)

'97 PROBE GT. The Probe never fulfilled its hope for Ford as a modern front-wheel-drive replacement for the Mustang. Production in its ninth and final year in both $14,280 coupe and $16,780 GT coupe versions came to only 16,821, compared to the 100,250 chalked up by Mustang. Probe shared engines, transmissions, and other mechanical components with Mazda, Ford's Japanese affiliate. (N.)

'97 MUSTANG CONVERTIBLE. This is a rear view of a 1997 $20,755 Mustang base V-6 convertible. The rear styling is basically unchanged since the introduction of the 1994 car, and was destined not to change until the introduction of the restyled 1999 Mustang. Internally, the base V-6 gained five horsepower, to 150. The 4.6-liter V-8 in the Cobra series gained aluminum block and heads, rated at 305 horsepower, compared to 215 in the 4.6 in the GT. (N.)

'98 MUSTANG CONVERTIBLE. The 1998 Mustang GT pictured here is little changed in looks from the 1994 model that was first of the fourth-generation Mustangs. Distinguishing the GT from the base coupe and convertible are 16-inch wheels (compared to 15-inch wheels), spoiler on the rear deck, and (unseen) dual exhaust pipes for the GT's standard V-8. The base V-6 engine was tweaked for an additional 10 horsepower, to 225. Total production for the 1998 Mustang rose to 144,000. Restyling for the following year, 1999, and then a fifth-generation Mustang, were coming in the car's next decade. (N.)

'02 MUSTANG, REAR. For model years 1999 through 2004, fourth-generation Mustangs carried through the front and rear "New Edge" restyling introduced with 1999 models. In this book, a guide can be found by comparing the rear view of this '02 on a used car lot with the rear of a '97 (page 113, bottom). Taillight design is one easy way to identify a Mustang's vintage. (D.)

'01 BULLITT COBRA INSTRUMENT PANEL. Shown here is the cockpit of the 2001 Mustang "Bullitt" model produced in limited volume to mark the 1968 Hollywood movie's memorable chase scene. In the film, a 1968 Mustang GT 390 and a Dodge Charger were featured. Compare this image with that of the previous-generation Mustang on page 110. In 2008, Ford produced another Bullitt replica for sale to enthusiasts. (FC.)

'01 BULLITT COBRA TESTING. Pictured in this 2000 photograph is a prototype of the '01 Mustang Cobra Bullitt "memory" model undergoing road testing by Ford's Special Vehicles group. The Gen Four 2001 and Gen Five 2008 Bullitt "replicars" featured newer-design engines (contemporary 281-cid Modular V-8 versus old 390-cid FE series), transmissions, and suspensions inside bodies painted dark green and sparsely trimmed to resemble the automotive "movie star" of 1968. (FC.)

'01 MUSTANG GT. This glamour photograph shows a 2001 Mustang in action. The rear deck spoiler and the shape of the air scoop on the hood identify this as a GT series Mustang. Rival General Motors discontinued production of competitive cars Camaro and Firebird for eight years after 2002. Mustang's other rival, Dodge Challenger, was missing from the marketplace from 1984 to 2008. (FC.)

'02 MUSTANG. This is the front view of a 2002 base Mustang V-6 convertible, captured in 2013 at a Michigan Ford dealer's used car lot, an inevitable stop in the life of all automobiles that are not preserved as collector cars. This car is well preserved for an 11-year old model, and, with a modest asking price of $6,995, could well be on its way to someone's collection as a keeper. (D.)

'03 MUSTANG GT CONVERTIBLE. Here is an "official" Ford studio portrait of a 2003 Mustang GT convertible. It appears identical to 1999 through 2002 models in the next-to-last year of the generation introduced in 1994 and restyled for 1999. The differences were mainly inside, with upgraded base V-6 and new V-8 engines. The transition from pony cars to muscle cars was complete—especially for the base and GT series. (FC.)

'03 SVT COBRA. This is an official Ford Motor Company glamour photograph of a 2003 Mustang Cobra convertible, identified by the shape of the air scoop behind the driver door and the running lights located at either side of the front-end "chin" in the bumper area. In 1999, horsepower of the base V-6 had been tweaked to 190, then 193 for 2001. The Cobra V-8 was up to 390 horsepower in the '03 model shown. (FC.)

'03 MUSTANG MACH I. Another historic Ford "hot car" name returned for the 2003 and 2004 model years: Mach 1. This image of a 2003 model Mustang Mach 1 is from Ford's media website. The car was priced between the GT and Cobra series Mustangs that year. The most successful sales year for the 1994–2004 Mustangs was 169,200 in 2001. In 2003, US Mustang sales reached 140,350, in a year in which industry sales were up. (FC.)

Ten

GENERATIONS FIVE AND SIX MILLENNIAL MUSTANGS 2005–2015

MUSTANG'S 40TH BIRTHDAY. In April 2004, as a platform for teasing the media and loyal customers about the "all-new" 2005 Mustang, Ford joined with the Mustang Club of America for a Mustang 40th birthday party celebration at Nashville's Superspeedway. Seen in this photograph, taken from the top of the stadium, are just some of the 3,000 Mustangs from all over the country that registered to attend. (D.)

'05 MUSTANG TESTING. Ace Detroit automobile writer and spy photographer Jim Dunne grabbed this photograph of a well-disguised 2005 Mustang prototype under test. The paint scheme was an attempt by Ford folks to keep the appearance of the new model literally under wraps. Automobile enthusiast magazines and even daily newspapers readily pay for such catches many months before formal press releases and public introduction. (Jim Dunne.)

'05 MUSTANG ON ASSEMBLY LINE. A brand-new 2005 GT is driven off the final assembly line at Ford's Flat Rock, Michigan, plant, months before public introduction. Note the cartoon-like sawtooth camouflage on the Mustang's front end, designed—like the proliferation of spots on the Mustang above—to hide specific aspects of the car's appearance. This was among the first of the fifth-generation Mustangs. (FC.)

'05 MUSTANGS. Days and weeks before public introduction and sale, new models, such as these 2005 Mustang GTs, are made available to members of the media for "test drives," in the hopes of garnering favorable reports. All these early 2005 Mustangs appear to be the higher-priced and better-equipped GT model coupes, with few or no convertibles and no base models. These 2005 GTs follow tradition by having their auxiliary driving, or fog, lamps mounted within the grille. (FC.)

'06 MUSTANG, REAR. This rear view of a 2006 Mustang GT coupe shows the differences in appearance from earlier vintage Mustangs. The GT emblem is inserted into the center-rear gas cap. This GT model is also indicated by dual exhaust pipes, wheel designs, and the rear air spoiler on the deck lid. (FC.)

'05 GT Convertible and '07 Coupe, Front. These two Mustangs at a Michigan Cadillac dealership are a 2005 GT convertible (right) and a base '07 V-6 coupe. Fortunately for purposes of identification, the lot managers painted the Mustang model years on their windshields. (D.)

'05 GT Convertible and '07 Coupe, Rear. This is a rear shot of the same two used Mustangs shown above, the '05 GT convertible (left) and the base 2007 coupe. Other than the typical series differences, such as GT badges, labels, dual exhausts, and auxiliary headlamps, there are few if any appearance changes between the Mustangs two model years apart. (D.)

'06 MUSTANG. Here, a collector '06 Mustang coupe poses with a P-51 Mustang fighter aircraft. On page 81, a '70 Mustang is seen with the same airplane during a Shelby American Automobile Club program. A 1965 Mustang also posed with its namesake, but was not chosen for this book because the vehicle had been modified with nonstandard aftermarket wheels. Modifying or personalizing Mustangs, while popular, detracts from the value to purists. (L.)

'08 BULLITT REMEMBRANCE. This is the '08 Mustang created by Ford to capitalize on the public and enthusiast passion for the 1968 movie *Bullitt*, starring Steve McQueen. The movie is famous for its dramatic, four-and-a-half-minute chase scene through San Francisco streets as McQueen, playing a San Francisco police detective, pursues paid killers in a Dodge Charger. The reproduction is shown here in a typical 'Frisco street scene. The Bullitt emblem on a replicar is shown in the inset. (FC; inset, D.)

'11 MUSTANG. For 2010 Mustang models introduced in the spring of 2009, there were substantial front and rear appearance changes, as shown on these used 2011 models. They can be compared to earlier models (see page 122). The 2011 Mustang also had a new 305-horsepower, 3.72-liter (227-cid) aluminum block V-6 as base engine and, for GT, a new 32-valve 5.0 "Coyote" V-8 of 412 horsepower, plus new transmissions. (D.)

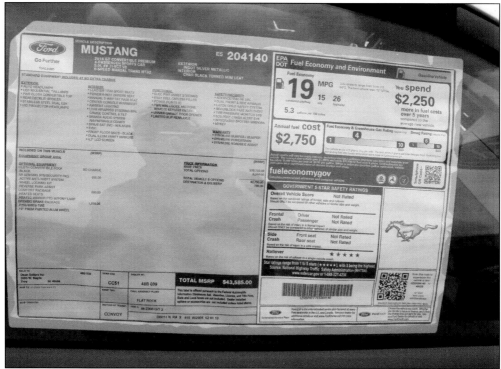

'14 MUSTANG PRICE STICKER. This price sticker on a new 2014 Mustang GT V-8 convertible at a Michigan Ford dealership shows the delivered price—subject to negotiation—of $43,585, including $3,040 for options. The price does not include destination and delivery charges, sales tax, or license. It was the most expensive Mustang in the dealer's inventory at the time. The lowest-price '14 Mustang at the dealer, a V-6 Premium coupe, carried a sticker price of $32,175. (D.)

'14 MUSTANG BASE. The 2014 base Six-cylinder 2014 coupe, pictured here at a Michigan Ford dealership, displays horizontal bars in its grille, true to the original '65 and especially the '66 models. Likewise, the size (footprint) remains much the same as the originals, though both price (see page 124) and weight have soared. General economic inflation, product improvements (including more standard equipment), and mandated government regulations account for the higher price. (D.)

'14 MUSTANG GT. Shown here are the front and rear of a 2014 Mustang GT convertible, awaiting delivery at a Ford Motor Company storage lot in Dearborn. Note the Mustang GT cues: driving lights within the grille at the front and, at the rear, the deck-lid spoiler, gas cap GT identification, and dual exhausts. The fore-and-aft racing stripes shown on the similar model on the previous page were part of an extra-cost option. (D.)

'14 SHELBY COBRA. This view of the rear panel of a 2014 Shelby Cobra shows clearly that the car is not a Mustang, carrying instead the "Shelby" brand name above the tail lamps and gas cap. In addition, the cobra symbol appears, in place of the traditional script-in-oval Ford emblem or Mustang badge. Legendary racer and race car builder Carroll Shelby had worked with Ford (and Chrysler) for years, designing modified, limited-production, high-performance cars before his death in 2012 at age 89. (D.)

'14 COBRA CONVERTIBLE. This 2014 Shelby Cobra GT500 convertible awaits delivery to a Ford Motor Company executive near the firm's world headquarters, seen in the background. The '14 Cobra has the same overall dimensions as a regular production Mustang, but offers a 662-horsepower, supercharged 5.8-liter V-8, other performance enhancements, and special trim—all for a price that can approach $70,000. (D.)

Sixth-Generation '15 Mustang. This is a sixth-generation, 2015 Mustang fastback coupe. This photograph was released at a sneak preview for suppliers, dealers, employees, and media in December 2013. The 50th anniversary 'Stang was scheduled to go on sale in the fall of 2014, to be joined by a convertible version several weeks later. In 2015, Ford plans to make Mustang fully global, marketed in many additional countries with right-hand drive versions, built on the same Flat Rock, Michigan, assembly line as the conventional North American left-hand drive car. The domestic car would be offered with three engine choices: a new 2.3-liter EcoBoost Four; a carryover 3.7-liter V-6; and a new 5.0-liter V-8. The newest Mustang is mounted on a 107-inch wheelbase, an inch shorter than the original 1965 model, but with a wider rear tread to accommodate independent rear suspension, a first for the full car line, designed to provide better ride and handling and also extra trunk space. (FC.)

BIBLIOGRAPHY

Fria, Robert A. *Mustang Genesis: The Creation of the Pony Car.* Jefferson, NC: McFarland & Company Inc., 2010.

Lamm, Michael, and Dave Holls. *A Century of Automotive Style: 100 Years of American Car Design.* Stockton, CA: Lamm-Morada Publishing Company, 1996.

Standard Catalogue of American Cars, 1805–1942. 1st Ed. Iola, WI: Krause Publications, 1985.

Standard Catalogue of American Cars, 1946–1975. 1st Ed. Iola, WI: Krause Publications, 1987.

Standard Catalogue of American Cars, 1976–1999. 1st Ed. Iola, WI: Krause Publications, 1987.

Standard Catalogue of Imported Cars, 1946–2002. 2nd Ed. Iola, WI: Krause Publications, 2002.

www.wikipedia.org. "Mustang," "Camaro," and "Challenger."

DISCOVER THOUSANDS OF LOCAL HISTORY BOOKS
FEATURING MILLIONS OF VINTAGE IMAGES

Arcadia Publishing, the leading local history publisher in the United States, is committed to making history accessible and meaningful through publishing books that celebrate and preserve the heritage of America's people and places.

Find more books like this at
www.arcadiapublishing.com

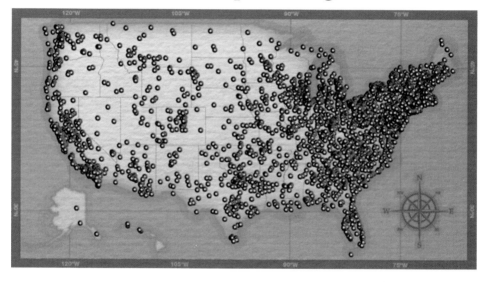

Search for your hometown history, your old stomping grounds, and even your favorite sports team.